The Tros

G. E. Mitton

Alpha Editions

This edition published in 2024

ISBN : 9789362092182

Design and Setting By
Alpha Editions
www.alphaedis.com
Email - info@alphaedis.com

Contents

CHAPTER I

"THE LADY OF THE LAKE"

THE charm that lies in a mysterious name has been amply exemplified in that of the Trossachs, which is said to mean "bristled territory." Something in the shaggy uncouthness of the word fits so well with the land of romance and mountain scenery that it has drawn tens of thousands to make the round between Glasgow and Edinburgh, by rail and coach and steamer, who, if the name had not been so mysteriously attractive, might never have bestirred themselves at all. Since the publication of *Rob Roy* and *The Lady of the Lake* the principal actors in these dramas have been just as real and important to the imaginative tourist as the familiar names of history. It is nothing to them that Rob Roy, of the clan of Macgregor, was merely a Highland thief: his character, invested by Scott with the charm of a magician's pen, has made him as heroic as the great Wallace himself; while Ellen, the Lady of the Lake, wholly born of the poet's imagination, has become only second to Mary Queen of Scots.

Scott has certainly done much for the land of his birth: not only has he enriched its literature for all time, and raised its literary standing in the eyes of nations, but he has done more for it commercially than almost any other writer has ever done for any country in bringing to it streams of visitors, especially from across the Atlantic. The gold flowing from the coffers of the Sassenach into the pouches of the Gael is a perennial blessing which could hardly have been secured in any other way.

> "The Lady of the Lake"

We are told that on the appearance of *The Lady of the Lake*, "the whole country rang with the praises of the poet; crowds set off to view the scenery of Loch Katrine, till then comparatively unknown; and as the book came out just before the season for excursions, every house and inn in that neighbourhood was crammed with a constant succession of visitors. From the date of the publication of *The Lady of the Lake*, the post-horse duty in Scotland rose in an extraordinary degree, and it continued to do so for a number of years, the author's succeeding works keeping up the enthusiasm for our scenery which he had originally created."

There are fairer spots in Scotland than the Trossachs, beautiful as they are; yet, notwithstanding this, their popularity remains unabated. The trip certainly has the advantage of being accessible; it can be "done" in a day from either Edinburgh or Glasgow, and this is a great recommendation to those who are going on to "do" Europe in record time. Then, again, anyone who has seen Edinburgh and the Trossachs is fairly safe in saying he has seen Scotland, whereas one of wider range, who had, say, gone up the Highland Railway to Inverness and returned via the Caledonian Canal, if unmindful of the Trossachs, would be taunted with his omission every time the subject was mentioned.

However, the greatly increased facilities of steamer and rail do doubtless tend to send people farther afield, and the much longer round via the Caledonian Canal can count its hundreds where it previously counted units.

Until Scott's time the Trossachs were little known, but then the cult of scenery-worship as we know it had not been evolved. That they were somewhat known is shown in Dorothy Wordsworth's *Journal*.

When William Wordsworth, with his sister and the poet Coleridge, made a tour in 1803, they were met at Loch Katrine (coming from Loch Lomond) with stares of amusement from the peasants. "There were no boats," says Dorothy in her *Journal*, "and no lodging nearer than Callander, ten miles beyond the foot of the lake. A laugh was on every face when William said we were come to see the Trossachs; no doubt they thought we had better have stayed at our own homes. William endeavoured to make it appear not so very foolish by informing them that it was a place much celebrated in England, though perhaps little thought of by them." This was six years before the publication of the great poem.

The Trossachs proper are the irregularly-shaped hills and rocks, covered with a thick growth of bristling firs, that lie between Loch Katrine and Loch Vennachar, and along the shores of little Loch Achray. But the name is generally taken to mean the whole round, including the traversing of Loch Lomond, as well as Loch Katrine, and the road journey.

"BENEATH THE CRAGS OF BEN VENUE."

The precipitous ascents from the south-east corner of Loch Katrine.

Much the most usual route is from either Glasgow or Edinburgh, via Callander; but a secondary one, which has great attraction for some people, is that by Aberfoyle, which cuts into the heart of the Trossachs from the south. This has the disadvantage of missing Loch Vennachar; but, truth to tell, the coach drive along by Loch Vennachar is not beautiful, and were it not illumined by romantic imagination, and regarded as a prelude or epilogue to something better, it could easily be dispensed with.

The outline of the story of *The Lady of the Lake* is supposed to be known to everyone, but there are few who could give it off-hand. The principal character, and the only one not fictitious, is that of James V. of Scotland, and his habit of wandering incognito among his people is used to further the plot. The poem opens with a stag-hunt, when the fine animal, after leading his pursuers a tremendous dance, plunges into the Trossachs and disappears from view. Only one horseman has been able to follow up the chase, and his steed at this juncture drops down dead, leaving his master to scramble onward to Loch Katrine as best he can. This he does, and as he stands on the shore he sees a boat rowed by a young girl rapidly approaching, coming out from a little island. She tells him he is expected—in fact, his visit has been foretold by a soothsayer, Allan Bane—and asks him to come to the island and receive the hospitality of her father's house. She is Ellen, daughter to one of the outlawed Douglases, who have been in arms against their King.

The girl's mother receives the stranger courteously on his arrival, and he announces himself as James Fitz-James. He remains with them that night, and leaves next morning before the return of Douglas with Ellen's young lover, Malcolm Graeme, and a powerful rebel, Roderick Dhu, the head of Clan MacAlpine, the Macgregors.

An outlawed desperate man,

The chief of a rebellious clan.

This man tries to gain Ellen's hand as the price of his support of her father, but his suit is unsuccessful.

The Fiery Cross

The next day, determined on a wild rising against the King, who is known to be at Stirling with his Court, Roderick sends the fiery cross round to summon his followers to Lanrick Mead. The cross is made by the priest—

A cubit's length in measure due,

The shaft and limbs were rods of yew.

This was dipped in the blood of a slaughtered goat and scathed with flame. Then the priest shook it on high, shouting:

"Woe to the wretch who fails to rear

At this dread sign the ready spear!

For, as the flames this symbol sear,

His home, the refuge of his fear,

A kindred fate shall know.

*   *   *   *   *

Sunk be his home in embers red!

And cursed be the meanest shed

That e'er shall hide the houseless head.

*   *   *   *   *

Burst be the ear that fails to heed!

Palsied the foot that shuns to speed!

May ravens tear the careless eyes,

Wolves make the coward heart their prize."

Roderick's servant, Malise, seizing the cross, starts off through the Trossachs, and along Loch Achray to Duncraggan, where he hands the symbol on to "Angus, heir of Duncan's line," who carries it along Vennachar and up to the pass of Leny, passing it on to a bridegroom on Loch Lubnaig, and so it follows round all the haunts of the clan.

Ellen and her father meantime retreat to a cave on Ben Venue. Here she accidentally meets again the fascinating stranger, who tries to persuade her to elope with him; but she tells him of her love for young Malcolm, and he honourably refrains from pressing his suit; instead he gives her a ring which, he says, was given him by the King, with a promise that on its production the King would fulfil any request of the wearer. Meantime he is being watched by Roderick Dhu as a spy, and Roderick sends a so-called guide to conduct him out of the labyrinth; but the guide is one of the clan Murdoch, who has secret orders to kill the stranger so soon as he gets him alone. The seer has proclaimed that whichever side first kills one of the other will win in the trial of strength now about to begin, and when Roderick hears this he rejoices to think that by treachery the lot will fall to him.

Fitz-James, however, is warned by a half-witted woman wandering in the wood, and when he discloses his suspicions he is shot at by Murdoch, who, however, misses him and kills the woman instead. Fitz-James, furious at this barbarity, promptly kills him, and, cutting off a tress of the dying woman's hair, swears to kill the chief, Roderick Dhu, the author of this foul deed, whenever he shall meet him. He wanders on in the wilderness of trees and rocks, and, as night is coming on, he loses himself.

Famished and chilled, through ways unknown,

Tangled and steep, he journeyed on;

Till, as a rock's huge point he turned,

A watch-fire close before him burned.

The Fight

Beside it is a huge Highlander, who is at first churlish and inclined to resent the intrusion; but the inbred virtue of hospitality conquers, and he allows the stranger to share his camp, promising to see him safe as far as Coilantogle Ford next morning. However, in the morning the two quarrel, and the great Highlander is revealed as Roderick Dhu himself. Roderick is furious at hearing of the death of Murdoch, but would have kept his word and given his guest safe-conduct had not Fitz-James, burning to be at him, absolved him from it, and they fight close by the ford. Just as Roderick is about to stab his foe mortally he himself sinks down, overcome with loss of blood, and some men-at-arms from Stirling ride up, greeting Fitz-James as the King. They carry the senseless body of Roderick back with them to Stirling.

When the King is once again in his own fortress games and sports take place, and Ellen's father, who has dared to attend them incognito, reveals himself in a burst of temper and is captured.

Ellen now makes her way to Stirling, carrying the ring, which proves an Open Sesame, and discovers to her astonishment the "knight in Lincoln green" who wooed her in the forest is no other than the monarch himself. James keeps his word, forgives her father, and pledges her to young Malcolm. Roderick, whose crimes would have made him difficult to pardon, conveniently dies, and the story finishes happily.

Scott in the Trossachs

Scott was very particular that the scenery of his plot should be correct, and visited the Trossachs carefully, and even rode from Loch Vennachar to Stirling, to make sure of the possibility of the feat he attributed to Fitz-James. In view of the warlike nature of the poem, Lockhart remarks it was rather an odd coincidence that the first time Scott entered the Trossachs he did so "riding in all the dignity of danger, with a front and rear guard and loaded arms, to enforce the execution of a legal instrument against some Maclarens, refractory tenants of Stewart of Appin."

CHAPTER II

THE ROYAL CITY OF STIRLING

AS a good deal of the scene of the poem is laid at Stirling, and as most people will take the opportunity of breaking their journey at so classic a town, a few pages must be devoted to it.

STIRLING CASTLE, FROM THE KING'S KNOT.

In 1304 the Castle was taken by the English after a three month's siege, and held by them until the Battle of Bannockburn in 1314.

The "Round Table"

The rock on which the castle of Stirling stands is a most remarkable object in the landscape, jutting out with the precipitousness of a sea-cliff from the plain. It is absolutely inaccessible on the one side, but slopes away on the other, and it is on these slopes that the town stands. Many a visitor has grumbled at the long pull up through the narrow, and in some places squalid, streets before reaching the castle; but the reward is great, for the view is far-reaching. It may be best seen, however, from a place called the Ladies' Rock in the churchyard, because there it includes the castle-rock on its steepest side. Here, also, there is to be found a plan of all the mountains by which they may be identified—Bens Ledi, Lomond, Vane, More, and Voirlich; also, down below, is a curious turf-garden, called the King's Knot, said to have been the scene of the mimic games and contests of the Court. It was here Scott laid the scene of the games described in the poem, and with what redoubled interest can the account be read, when, having seen the place, memory can conjure up a mind-picture of it! This odd terracing is mentioned by Barbour, in describing the flight of Edward II. after Bannockburn, as the Round Table. It is within the bounds of possibility that it existed in the days of King Arthur, for centuries before Arthur's time Stirling was a Roman station, and the King in his day is known to have been in the neighbourhood.

The history of Stirling reaches back beyond all records. Long before Edinburgh had attained its position as capital of the kingdom, while it was still but a Border fortress, liable to be taken and retaken as English or Scots extended their territory, Stirling was one of the strongholds of the country. From time immemorial some fortress had stood on this impregnable position. In 1124 Alexander I. died here, so that it must then have been a fortress-palace, and in 1304 the castle held out for three months against Edward I. of England. After it was taken it remained in the possession of England until the Battle of Bannockburn, and Bannockburn lies only about three miles from Stirling. Even the supine Edward II. wended his way so far north with the object of retaining such a desirable place. James III. was born here, and probably James IV. also, while James V., the hero of *The Lady of the Lake*, was crowned in the parish church as a toddling child of two. His much-discussed daughter, Queen Mary, passed the years of her childhood at the castle. Her little son James, who was destined to unite the two kingdoms, was baptized at the castle with tremendous ceremony, while his father, Darnley, sulked apart, and refused to take his proper position. Here James VI. and I. spent mainly the first thirteen years of his life, under the tutelage of the scholar George Buchanan, and it was only when he became King of England that Stirling ceased to be a royal residence.

Of the origin of the name Stirling there is no certain record. In old records it is spelt Stryveling, Strivilin, and so on, through various minor alterations, wherefore it has sometimes been held to mean "strife," a most appropriate signification. It used occasionally to be referred to also as Snowdon, a fact mentioned in Scott's poem:

For Stirling's Tower

Of yore the name of Snowdon claims.

The Wandering King

By far the most striking part of the castle is the palace, which was begun by James IV. and finished by James V. This is in the form of a square, and is decidedly French in character, a fact attributed to the influence of his wife, Mary of Guise. Strange life-size figures project beneath arcades, and the carving is in some cases most weird and grotesque. James V. was very much associated with the castle. He was fond of assuming disguises and wandering about incognito among his people; for this purpose he sometimes took the name of the "Gudeman of Ballengeich," Ballengeich being a road running below the castle walls. The songs "The Gaberlunzie Man" and "We'll gang nae mair a-rovin" are said to have been founded on his exploits. He was renowned for his success with the fair sex, and altogether the rôle given to him by Scott fits him admirably.

The castle is now occupied by a garrison, and the picturesque Highland dress of the men adds much as a foreground to the grey walls of the old buildings. An awkward squad may frequently be seen drilling in the courtyard, unkindly exposed to the eyes of passing visitors. In this square is the Parliament House, built by James III., and this is where the last Parliament in Scotland held its sittings.

The Douglas Room

The Douglas Room, reached by a narrow passage, will, however, claim most attention from those to whom history is a living thing. It was here that James II. stabbed the Earl of Douglas in 1452. The Douglases had so grown in power and influence, that it had begun to be a question whether Stuarts or Douglases should reign in Scotland. The King was afraid of the power of his mighty rivals, and accordingly invited the Douglas, the eighth Earl, to come as his guest to the castle for a conference. The Douglas came without misgiving, though it is said he demanded, and received, a safe-conduct. It was about the middle of January, and no doubt huge log fires warmed the inclement air in the great draughty halls where the party dined and supped with much appearance of cordiality and goodwill, but beneath lay hate and terror and rancour, bitter as the grave.

After supper the King drew Douglas aside to an inner chamber, and tried to persuade him to break away from the allies which threatened, with his house, to form a combination disastrous to the security of the throne. The Earl refused, and high words began to fly from one to the other. The King demanded that Douglas should break from his allies, and the Earl replied again he would not. "Then this shall!" cried the King, twice stabbing his guest with his own royal hand. Sir Patrick Grey, who was near by, came up and finished the job with a pole-axe, and then the body was thrown over into the court below. It was a gross violation of every law of decency even in those lawless days, and well the King must have known the storm his action would arouse. Burton, the historian of Scotland, adduces this as evidence that the crime was not meditated, but done in a mere fit of ungovernable rage. The murdered man's four brothers surrounded and besieged the castle, and nailing to a cross in contempt the safe-conduct the King had given, trailed it through the miry streets tied to the tail of the wretchedest horse they could find, thus publishing the ignominy of their Sovereign. They burnt and destroyed wherever they could, and the King had many years of strenuous warfare before him as a result of that night's work.

From the castle battlements the "bonny links of Forth" can be seen winding and looping and doubling on themselves, and also the old bridge, which was the key to the Highlands and the only dry passage across the Forth for centuries. This bridge is even older than any existing part of the castle. It has seen many desperate skirmishes, most notable of which was that of 1715, when the Duke of Argyll, with only 1,500 men, held here in check thousands of Highlanders. Here we must leave Stirling, without noting the rest of the old buildings, as this is no guide-book, and the city is merely looked upon as the key to the Trossachs and the scene of some of the drama enacted in *The Lady of the Lake*.

CHAPTER III

BY THE ROUTE OF THE FIERY CROSS TO BALQUHIDDER

FEW indeed of those who come up comfortably by rail to Callander, and step at once to a seat on a waiting four-horsed coach, adorned by a scarlet-coated driver and tootling horn, ever think of arriving a day sooner and exploring northward along the continuation of the single line which has brought them so far, or, better still, of going on northward by road through the Pass of Leny to beautiful little Strathyre for the night. Yet they miss much by not doing so, for at Balquhidder, a little beyond Strathyre, is the grave of Rob Roy and the reputed graves of his wife and son, while up the Pass of Leny itself was carried the fiery cross, so that the story of *The Lady of the Lake* is hardly complete without a visit to it.

Few more beautiful passes are to be seen than Leny. The dashing stream which runs in a wooded cleft below the road is exactly what one expects a Scottish stream to be. The brown peat-water breaks in cascades over huge grey weather-worn stones, or lies in deep clear pools. The irregularities of its course reveal new beauties at every turn: the dripping green ferns, for ever sprinkled with the spray, hang quivering over the agate depths, and the emerald moss, saturated like a sponge, softens the sharp angles of stones. Tufts of free-growing heather, large as bushes, add colour to the scene, and the slender white stems of the birches rise gracefully amid the gnarled alders and dark-needled firs. The Falls of Leny are reached by a footpath from the road.

Angus, carrying the cross, was confronted by the stream, which divided him from the chapel of St. Bride, whose site is now marked by a small graveyard just where the water issues from Loch Lubnaig. He had to plunge in, panting and hot as he was.

He stumbled twice—the foam splashed high,

With hoarser swell the stream raced by.

Then, gaining the shore, he faced the chapel entrance just as a gay crowd came forth escorting a newly-wedded pair.

LOCH VENNACHAR.

Here was Coilantogle Ford where King James V. fought Roderick Dhu.

In rude but glad procession came

Bonneted sire and coif-clad dame;

And plaided youth with jest and jeer,

Which snooded maiden would not hear.

The Bridegroom's Part

Scott does not tell us why the dripping youth selected the bridegroom out of all the crowd to carry on the brand, but doubtless there were reasons: it was possibly his right as a senior in the clan. Still, it is little wonder that the unfortunate man, who dared not refuse, yet hesitated.

Yet slow he laid his plaid aside

And, lingering, eyed his lovely bride

Until he saw the starting tear

Speak woe he might not stop to cheer;

Then trusting not a second look,

In haste he sped him up the brook.

*   *   *   *   *

Mingled with love's impatience came

The manly thirst for martial fame.

*   *   *   *   *

Stung by such thoughts, o'er bank and brae

Like fire from flint he glanced away.

The railway crosses the stream about this point, and continues up the west side of the loch, while the road keeps on the right, or eastern, side. The rail passes Laggan Farm, said to be the birthplace of Rob's Amazonian wife, Helen, who takes a part only second to himself in the reader's imagination. Passing along, therefore, on either side we come, soon after the head of the loch, to bonny little Strathyre, lying amid its great hills, which are flushed as if with fire when the setting sun catches the sweep of the heather in season.

Only a few miles beyond Strathyre is Balquhidder, lying on the road to Loch Voil. The loch lies in a very beautiful situation at the foot of the range known as the Braes of Balquhidder, culminating in Ben A'an and Ben More. It is on the property of Mr. Carnegie, whose house, Stronvar, is at the east side. In the adventurous journey made by the Wordsworths in the beginning of the nineteenth century, they actually walked over the mountains to Balquhidder from Loch Katrine by a wild, rough track, and at the foot of the hills waded through the river. Dorothy thus describes the scenery: "The mountains all round are very high; the vale pastoral and unenclosed, not many dwellings and but a few trees; the mountains in general smooth near the bottom. They are in large unbroken masses, combining with the vale to give an impression of bold simplicity."

LOCH LUBNAIG.

It was at the end of this loch that Angus handed the Fiery Cross to the Bridegroom.

There were a few reapers in the fields, and it was from this fact that Wordsworth was inspired to write his poem *The Solitary Reaper*. The brother and sister visited the graves at Balquhidder before passing on to Callander.

It is said that when the freebooter Rob Roy lay dying in his own house at Balquhidder, his wife mocked at his repentance. He rebuked her, saying: "You have put strife betwixt me and the best men of the country, and now you would place enmity between me and my God."

Rob Roy's Grave

The grave of Rob Roy is in the little old graveyard, and is only a few feet from the gate. There are rude sculptured figures on the flat stone, seemingly far older than the days of the freebooter, but possibly an old stone was used to mark the place where he at length rested after his roving life. This is not the only association that Balquhidder evokes, for it is mentioned in *The Legend of Montrose*, when the Clan Macgregor there agree to stand by the murderers of the King's deer-keeper; and also in more modern fiction, when, in Stevenson's *Kidnapped*, poor David breaks down utterly at Balquhidder, and has to be guarded and cared for by his quaint comrade, Alan Breck.

But, tempting as it is to wander farther up the glen, here we must stop, or we shall get too far from our legitimate route through the Trossachs.

CHAPTER IV

APPROACHES TO THE TROSSACHS

THE route taken by the coaches leaves Callander in a northward direction, but soon turns off westward down a narrow muddy road forbidden to motor-cars; this runs beneath the shoulder of Ben Ledi.

Ben Ledi means the Mount of God, and is believed to have been held sacred from the days when the Beltane mysteries were celebrated on it. Beltane was a Celtic festival celebrated about May 1 with fires and dances, and probably with sacrifices too. The scenery, however, is not as awe-inspiring as these weird memories would lead one to expect—in fact, for all this first part of the Trossachs' round the traveller's imagination must supply all the fire he needs. For instance, the very prosaic sluices erected by the Glasgow Water Company at the end of Loch Vennachar, which soon comes into view, mark the site of Coilantogle Ford, across which Roderick promised the King a safe-conduct, and where the two fought with such fury when the outlaw revealed himself.

The chief in silence strode before,

And reach'd that torrent's sounding shore

Which, daughter of three mighty lakes,

From Vennachar in silver breaks.

The road passes all along the shores of Loch Vennachar, and where at the end there lies a meadow, embraced on the far side by the Finlas Water, we are at another classic spot, for this is Lanrick Mead, the meeting-place of the Macgregor clansmen. We can see very well why it should have been chosen, for it guards at its narrowest part the pass, and anyone approaching from the Callander—*i.e.*, the Doune or Stirling direction—would be easily stopped, though it would be possible for men to come along the south side of Lochs Vennachar and Achray. The mead also commands the approach from the south via Aberfoyle, and any body of men coming down the hill on this side would be full in view. After this we arrive at the Brig o' Turk, a small bridge over the Finlas Water. It was close by here, at a few huts marking Duncraggan, that Malise delivered up the cross to Angus. But he had done his work well.

The fisherman forsook the strand,

The swarthy smith took dirk and brand;

With changèd cheer the mower blithe

Left in the half-cut swathe the scythe;

The herds without a keeper stray'd,

The plough was in mid-furrow staid,

The falc'ner tossed his hawk away,

The hunter left the stag at bay;

Prompt at the signal of alarms,

Each son of Alpine rush'd to arms.

BRIG O' TURK AND BEN VENUE.

In the great stag hunt, with which Scott's poem opens, it was at this point that "the headmost horseman rode alone."

We are now right in the Trossachs proper, and find the huge, palatial hotel which goes by that name facing little Loch Achray.

Having arrived at the junction of the roads—that is, the two principal approaches already noted—it is necessary to run over the ground from Aberfoyle before continuing the part through the Trossachs common to both routes.

Aberfoyle

Aberfoyle itself is full of associations, but they are nearly all connected with *Rob Roy*. It stands as a meeting-place of Highlands and Lowlands, and as such has seen many storms. The earlier part of the Forth, here known as the Laggan, runs past the town, and the old saying "Forth bridles the wild Highlandman" is full of significance. Of this district says Mr. Cunninghame Graham: "Nearly every hill and strath has had its battles between the Grahames and the Macgregors. Highlander and Lowlander fought in the lonely glens or on the stony hills, or drank together in the aqua-vitæ houses in the times of their precarious peace."

Far the most interesting scene laid at Aberfoyle, in all the realism of fiction, is that in *Rob Roy*, when Bailie Nicol Jarvie, and young Osbaldistone arrived, wearied out, seeking shelter at the primitive Clachan, and were refused because "three Hieland shentlemens" wanted the place to themselves. The landlady said her house was taken up "wi' them wadna like to be intruded on wi' strangers," an objection for which there was probably strong underlying reason!

The row that subsequently took place when the stout little Bailie defended himself with the red-hot coulter of a plough is too well known to need quotation. Suffice it to say, in evidence of the truth of the story, that a coulter, traditionally said to be the very weapon, hangs on a tree outside the hotel, which bears his name, to this very day.

IN THE HEART OF THE TROSSACHS.

The Pass of Aberfoyle

The pass which leads by Lochs Ard and Chon north-westward to Stronachlachar has been much used at all times, and has seen desperate forays, but none perhaps more desperate than that described in *Rob Roy* when the Bailie and Osbaldistone, unwillingly setting forth up it with an escort of soldiery, were attacked from the heights above by the redoubtable Helen Macgregor and her men, and very narrowly escaped death. Scott thus describes the pass:

"Our route, though leading toward the lake, had hitherto been so much shaded by wood that we only from time to time obtained a glimpse of that beautiful sheet of water. But the road now suddenly emerged from the forest ground, and, winding close by the margin of the loch, afforded us a full view of its spacious mirror, which now, the breeze having totally subsided, reflected in still magnificence the high dark heathy mountains, huge grey rocks and shaggy banks, by which it is encircled. The hills now sank on its margin so closely, and were so broken and precipitous, as to afford no passage except just upon the narrow line of the track which we occupied and which was overhung with rocks, from which we might have been destroyed merely by rolling down stones, without much possibility of offering resistance. Add to this that as the road winded round every promontory and bay which indented the lake, there was rarely a possibility of seeing a hundred yards before us."

It was when the party had reached a spot where the path rose in zigzags and made its slippery way across the face of a steep slaty cliff that they suddenly discovered they were in an ambuscade under the command of Helen Macgregor herself. The desperate fight that followed, all in favour of the outlaws who commanded the situation; the ludicrous plight of the fat little Bailie, who, caught by the back of the coat on a projecting thorn-bush, swung in mid-air, "where he dangled not unlike the sign of the Golden Fleece over the door of a mercer in the Trongate of his native city"—are not these things writ in the ever-enduring pages of *Rob Roy*? More awful was the doom of Morris the Gauger, or Exciseman, who was dragged out, condemned as a spy, and drowned by the aid of a large stone bound in a plaid about his neck. "Half naked and thus manacled, they hurled him into the lake, there about twelve feet deep, with a loud halloo of vindictive triumph, above which, however, his last death shriek, the yell of mortal agony, was distinctly heard."

The lake thus woven into the tale is supposed to be Loch Ard. The Falls of Ledard, at the north-western end, are the falls described by Scott in *Waverley*, as he himself has owned, though it must be confessed in so doing he lifted them from their setting. Flora MacIvor's song—

There is mist on the mountain and night on the vale,

But more dark is the sleep of the sons of the Gael

—is descriptive of this scenery.

"Rebels and Mossers"

But the Pass of Aberfoyle has scenes of real history to tell as well as those of fiction. General Monk led his men through it after addressing a letter to the Earl of Airth, desiring him to have the woods in certain districts of Aberfoyle cut down, because they were "grete shelters to the rebels and mossers."

In the pass, also, the Earl of Glencairn and Graham of Duchray defeated some of the Cromwellian soldiers, and, adds Mr. Cunninghame Graham in recounting the incident, "Graham of Duchray no doubt fought all the better because the Cromwellians had burnt his house the night before the action, in order to show him that it was unwise to attach too much importance to mere houses built with hands."

Aberfoyle is supposed to be peculiarly haunted by the "little folk"—*i.e.*, the fairies—a reputation it gained from a seventeenth-century minister, who was supposed to be in league with them. He is frequently mentioned by Scott, and the fairy knowe, opposite the hotel, on which he sank down dead, called back to the fairyland he loved so well, is still pointed out. He,

When the roaring Garry ran

Red with the life-blood of Dundee,

When coats were turning, crowns were falling,

Wandered along his valley still,

And heard their mystic voices calling

From fairy knowe and haunted hill.

Lake of Menteith

Not less interesting than the west side is the country lying east of Aberfoyle, where, at about an equal distance, is the lake of Menteith. As significant of the wildness of the place in bygone days, we may note that one Earl of Menteith declared war against "all but the kinge and those of the name of Grahame." Menteith was from earliest times one of the five great districts into which Scotland was divided. The Earls of Menteith (Grahams) were ever at feud with the warlike Macgregors, and, as often happens, the feuds raged worst just on the borders of the Highlands, where men might attack and retreat in safety, knowing every track which led into their wild fastnesses.

The lake of Menteith is about two miles by one, and it is curious to note this is the only *lake* in Scotland. On it is an island, where the Earls had their residence. Another island, called Inchmahone, is, however, more interesting still. The word means "Isle of Rest," and such it was found by the monks who lived here in ages long gone past. Ruins are left, a moulded doorway, a fine monument, to tell of their occupation, but "gone are the Augustinian monks who built the stately island church. Out of the ruined chancel grows a plane-tree, which is almost ripe. In the branches rooks have built their nests, and make as cheerful matins as perhaps the monks themselves. The giant chestnuts, grown, as tradition says, from chestnuts brought from Rome, are all stag-headed. Ospreys used to build in them in the memory of those still living. Gone are the 'Riders of Menteith' (if they ever existed); the ruggers and the reivers are at one with those they harried. The Grahams and Macgregors, the spearmen and the jackmen, the hunters and the hawkers, the livers by their spurs, the luckless Earls of Menteith and their retainers, are buried and forgotten, and the tourist cracks his biscuit and his jest over their tombs" (Cunninghame Graham).

The "Riders of Menteith" are spoken of in history, but whether, as Mr. Graham asks, they were mortal riders or a sort of *Walküren*, sacred to the Valhalla of the district, history does not enlighten us.

The Four Maries

Queen Mary, as a little girl of five, was brought to the island of Inchmahone after the Battle of Pinkie, and lived here for a whole year, until she went to France to be betrothed to the Dauphin. Her childish dreams beneath the great chestnuts can have contained no shadow of the stormy life and fearful end that awaited her. She was even at that time accompanied by the "four Maries" who attended on her, one of whom, Mary Hamilton, met the tragic fate of execution.

Last nicht there were four Maries,

This nicht there'll be but three:

There was Mary Beaton and Mary Seaton,

And Mary Carmichael and me.

The road from Aberfoyle to the Trossachs rises very steeply past some slate-quarries. As we rise the hills come into view—Ben Ledi and Ben Venue, with

Ben Lomond dominating all the landscape; Ben Voil peeping over Ben Lawers; and on the clearest days, far in the distance, Ben Nevis, Schiehallion, and many others. Far below to the right lies Loch Drunkie, and much nearer the desolate little tarn called Loch Reoichte, which signifies "frozen," and this among them all for desolate beauty stands first. Close by the road is a drinking-fountain, called "Rob Roy's Well," where the tourist is invited to slake his thirst, though the real well, to which the tradition attaches, is away from the road, above the slate-quarries on Craig Vadh. On the ridge of this same Craig Vadh, by the way, are curious cairns, covering the spot where the bodies of those slain in a Border foray were found. When the road at length descends we have the pleasing duty of paying an impost, or toll, for the use of it—and by no means a low one either—and thus we come to Loch Achray and the Trossachs Hotel, and pick up the thread where it was dropped.

CHAPTER V

THE HEART OF THE TROSSACHS

AS we have heard the Trossachs signifies "bristled territory," a suitable name enough, and as they have been described by the master himself, there would be little use in trying to improve upon his words, which are as follows:

With boughs that quaked at every breath,

Grey birch and aspen wept beneath;

Aloft, the ash and warrior oak

Cast anchor in the rifted rock;

And, higher yet, the pine-tree hung

His shattered trunk, and frequent flung,

Where seem'd the cliffs to meet on high,

His boughs athwart the narrow'd sky.

Highest of all where white peaks glanced,

Where glistening streamers waved and danced,

The wanderer's eye could barely view

The summer heaven's delicious blue;

So wondrous wild, the whole might seem

The scenery of a fairy dream.

Dorothy Wordsworth

It must be remembered that the beautiful even road which now runs through the heart of this fairyland was a work of great difficulty and cost. It has been hewn out of the side of the rock, and built up by the side of the loch in order to facilitate the constant stream of tourists. At first there were several wild pathways leading down to Loch Katrine through a perfect wilderness of boughs and undergrowth, and at the end a precipitous drop over the edge of a steep crag, only scaled by the aid of a sort of natural ladder of saplings and tendrils, and it is thus that Scott makes Fitz-James approach the loch. In the beginning of the nineteenth century, however, when Dorothy Wordsworth and her brother reached the Trossachs from Loch Katrine, a great improvement had taken place. When nearing the end of the lake, she says, they came in sight of two huts, which had been built by Lady Perth as a shelter for visitors. "The huts stand at a small distance from each other, on a high and perpendicular rock, that rises from the bed of the lake. A road, which has a very wild appearance, has been cut through the rock; yet even here, among these bold precipices, the feeling of excessive beautifulness overcomes every other."

THE SILVER STRAND, LOCH KATRINE.

Where Scott describes the meeting between Fitz-James and Ellen of the Isle.

In her there was already that new appreciation of the natural beauty which her brother was to do so much to encourage in all. Her description of the Trossachs, after they had landed, clearly shows this: "Above and below us, to the right and to the left, were rocks, knolls, and hills, which, whenever anything could grow—and that was everywhere between the rocks—were covered with trees and heather. The trees did not in any place grow so thick as an ordinary wood, yet I think there was never a bare space of twenty yards; it was more like a natural forest, where the trees grow in groups or singly, not hiding the surface of the ground, which, instead of being green and mossy, was of the richest purple. The heather was indeed the most luxuriant I ever saw; it was so tall that a child of ten years old struggling through it would often have been buried head and shoulders, and the exquisite beauty of the colour, near or at a distance, seen under the trees is not to be conceived."

And as it was then so it is now: a better description of the peculiar scenery of the Trossachs could hardly be given, especially if we add the detail that bog-myrtle and birches grow abundantly, adding to the fragrance and poetry of the place. Winding round to the right runs the road to the Silver Strand, now much covered by the rising of the water owing to the precautions taken by the Glasgow Waterworks, which gets its supply from Loch Katrine. Here Fitz-James is supposed to have stood. Right in front is Ellen's Isle, thickly wooded; behind it rises the vast shoulder of Ben Venue, and away to the right stretches westward the full length of the lake, broken by promontories,

Where, gleaming with the setting sun,

One burnish'd sheet of living gold,

Loch Katrine lay beneath him roll'd;

In all her length far winding lay,

With promontory, creek and bay,

And islands that, empurpled bright,

Floated amid the livelier light;

And mountains, that like giants stand,

To sentinel enchanted land.

High on the south, huge Ben Venue

Down to the lake in masses threw

Crags, knolls, and mounds, confusedly hurl'd,

The fragments of an earlier world.

In the whole of a justly celebrated poem there is no passage finer than this, and, oft quoted as it has been, it would be impossible to omit it.

Ellen's Isle is, of course, so named after Scott's heroine; the Highland name is Eilean Molach, meaning the "Shaggy Island," and it is quite likely that with this in his mind Scott chose the name Ellen as the nearest English-sounding equivalent.

The Goblin's Cave, to which Ellen and her family retreated, is on the side of Ben Venue, and above is the Bealach Nambo, or the Pass of the Cattle, which Scott alluded to as:

The dell upon the mountain's crest

Yawned like a gash on warrior's breast.

This can be reached on foot by a not too difficult walk, but most people prefer to view it from below. The Goblin's Cave is impossible of exact identification, if, indeed, it had any actual prototype.

Loch Katrine

It has been suggested that the name of Loch Katrine arose from the hordes of robbers, or caterans, who infested its shores. If this be so, the name has been softened into something much more appropriate to the loveliness of the scenery, which is at its best at the east end. The Wordsworth party, indeed, coming from the other end, were at first disappointed. As the only means of transit was by a small row-boat, Coleridge was afraid of the cold and walked along the northern shore from Glengyle, though not, of course, on the well-made-up road which runs part of the way at present. Wordsworth himself slept in the bottom of the boat, which they had procured with much difficulty, and told his sister to awake him if anything worth seeing occurred. It was not until they nearly reached the eastern end that she did this, though then she confessed that what they saw was "the perfection of loveliness and beauty."

The lake is about eight miles long by three-quarters broad, but the actual width varies very much, owing to the numerous indentations. The road on the northern shore runs to Glengyle, but there stops, so that the only means of getting right on to Loch Lomond is to take the steamer, which awaits tourists several times daily. No doubt a road by which cyclists could travel on their own account would be strenuously resisted in the neighbourhood, where the chief aim and object of the tourist's being is supposed to be to pay for everything. On the southern side the steepness of the precipices of Ben Venue prevents any possibility of a road.

LOCH KATRINE AND ELLEN'S ISLE.

Opposite to Ben Venue, and best seen from the lake itself, is Ben A'an, only 1,750 feet in height. At the north-west end of Loch Katrine is Glengyle, the hereditary burial-place of the Macgregors.

The steamer stops at Stronachlachar, about three-quarters of the way down the lake on the south side, and here a coach meets it to convey passengers across to Inversnaid, on Loch Lomond.

"Stepping Westward"

With Loch Katrine the scenes identified with *The Lady of the Lake* come to an end. The road to Loch Lomond passes over a wild, rough heath, in strong contrast to the wooded loveliness of the eastern end of Loch Katrine, but quite as attractive to some natures, especially when the soft grey clouds lie low and the russets and browns of the bracken and heather replace the rich glory of its purple robe. It was hereabouts that the Wordsworths, when returning to Lomond, were greeted by two Highland women, who said in a friendly way: "What! you are stepping westward"—a simple sentence which gave Wordsworth the inspiration for the poem which he wrote long afterwards beginning with the same words.

Loch Arklet lies very flat between its shores, and has no beauty except its wildness. At one end lived for some time Rob Roy and his wife; indeed, all this district, right up to Glen Falloch on the one side, and down to the shoulders of Ben Lomond on the other, is associated with the outlaw, of whom Scott made a hero. The district has also associations with a much greater than he, for it is redolent of the wanderings of Robert the Bruce, when he was hunted by his bitter enemies, the men of Lorn.

It is supposed that Roderick Dhu in Scott's poem was a shadowy form of Rob Roy, who is more developed in the book which was published seven years later. Both were of uncommon personal strength, both were cattle-lifters and outlaws, both were of the great clan of Macgregor, and there are minor resemblances.

BEN A'AN (Seen from Loch Katrine).

Rob's designation was "of Inversnaid," and he owned Craig Royston, a district lying east of Lomond, near the north end. He began as a man of property and a land-holder, rough and poor as his territory was. He went on to be a cattle-dealer on a large scale, and this turned to something more nefarious. A distraint was levied on his property, and he had to leave the shores of Lomond. To this fact is attributed the wild piper's tune of "The Lament of Rob Roy," composed by his wife, which has something of the mournful beauty of the country incorporated in its weird strains:

Through the depths of Loch Lomond the steed shall career,

O'er the heights of Ben Lomond the galley shall steer,

And the rocks of Craig Royston like icicles melt,

Ere our wrongs be forgot, or our vengeance unfelt.

Rob seems to have been in some way a Robin Hood, exercising generosity toward those poorer and weaker than himself, and he was greatly beloved by the people in consequence. Many a ballad is connected with his name, and he became a popular hero even before his death. He took part in 1715 Rebellion on the Jacobite side, and at the Battle of Sheriffmuir seems to have been afflicted with the peculiar indecision that paralyzed both sides on that memorable day. He was leading, beside his own clan, a party of Macphersons, whose chief was too infirm to take the field, and he retained his station on a hill, though positively ordered by the Earl of Mar to charge. It is said that this charge might have decided the day. This incident is embodied in the ballad on the occasion:

Rob Roy he stood watch

On a hill for to catch

The booty for aught that I saw, mon;

For he ne'er advanced

From the place where he stanced

Till nae mair was to do there at a', mon.

It is impossible to give even an account of all Rob's pranks, some of which are doubtless mythical, and others which do not greatly redound to his credit. He had certainly that picturesque personality which has attracted romancers in all ages, and he formed a very fitting subject for Scott's pen.

In the end he turned Roman Catholic, and died, as already stated, at Balquhidder.

The road drops very steeply down to Lomond, and passes the earthworks which mark the site of a fort built by William III. to overawe the rebels. The fort, being on the great outlaw's property, was an object of peculiar hatred. Twice it was surprised and taken—once by Roy himself and once by his nephew. It is said that at one time General, then Captain, Wolfe was in command of it.

The Highland Girl

The little stream Arklet dances and brawls over its bed, in its descent accompanying the road, and at length leaps into the lake by a splendid waterfall thirty feet in height. Close by this is the palatial hotel at Inversnaid, a brother to the one at the Trossachs. When the Wordsworths arrived here the first time, after having with great difficulty got across Loch Lomond in a row-boat, they found only a miserable ferry-house, with a mud floor, and rain coming in at the roof. It was here that Wordsworth saw the prototype of his "sweet Highland girl."

CHAPTER VI

LOMOND AND THE MACGREGORS

Ben Lomond

LOMOND is one of the two most magnificent lochs in Scotland. It is twenty-one miles long, its only rival being Loch Awe, which is three miles longer. It is of a curious wedge shape, being about five miles broad at the low end and narrowing to a point in the north. In the widest part it bears a perfect archipelago of islands, once thickly populated, but now left mostly to deer and other wild creatures. There is a tradition of a floating island, repeated by many an ancient traveller; but all trace of this phenomenon has vanished—if, indeed, it ever existed. The fishing in the loch is free, and salmon, sea-trout, lake-trout, pike, and perch are to be caught. The nearness of the great lake to Glasgow is at once an advantage and a drawback. It is an advantage for the thousands that pour out of the grimy city on every holiday, and, at half an hour from their own doors, for a trifling sum, can spend joyous days in scenery which can be classed with the most beautiful in the world. But it is certainly not an unmixed joy to the real lover of Nature, who approaches the lake in a spirit of worship, to find the shores black with people and the steamers thronged with tourists. The attractions pointed out to those who pass up or down the great sheet of water are various. Not the least is the giant Ben, who raises his proud head on the eastern side, "a sort of Scottish Vesuvius, never wholly without a cloud-cap. You cannot move a step that it does not tower over you. In winter a vast white sugar-loaf; in summer a prismatic cone of yellow and amethyst and opaline lights; in spring a grey, gloomy, stony pile of rocks; in autumn a weather indicator, for when the mist curls down its sides and hangs in heavy wreaths from its double summit, 'it has to rain,' as the Spaniards say."

The mountain is 3,192 feet high, and the ascent is not difficult; by the gradually sloping way from the hotel at Rowardennan it is about five or six miles, without any very stiff climbing, and there is a choice of other routes. On a clear day, which is a rare boon, the view from the summit is superb. Sitting on its topmost pinnacle, one looks down the almost perpendicular north-eastern slope into the little valley where the River Forth may be said to take its rise. On the western side Loch Lomond stretches out in full length, and across the narrow isthmus of Tarbet is the sea-loch, Loch Long. Far away to the east and south the eye may range over the Lothians, Edinburgh, and Arthur's Seat, and even to the distant hills of Cumberland and the Isle of Man; while farther west, backed by the Irish coast, is the whole scenery of the beautiful Clyde estuary and the nearer Hebrides. Northward, peak after peak, rise the stately masses of the Grampians.

Leaving Inversnaid, the first point to which attention is usually drawn is the cave in the corries on the east side, called Rob Roy's Cave; much farther down the loch, amid the screes of Ben Lomond, is another hole, called Rob Roy's Prison. The Island Vow, midway across the loch opposite Inversnaid, owes its name to a corruption of Eilean Vhow, meaning the Brownies' Isle, a fascinating enough name to a child. On the island are some remains of the Macfarlanes' stronghold. Wordsworth's poem *The Brownie* originated with this island. On the farther shore, a little more northward, there is what is called the Pulpit Rock, a cell cut out on the face of the cliff so that it could be used for open-air preaching.

The Macfarlanes

Right opposite is Ben Voirlich, and, in its fastnesses, wild Loch Sloy, whose name formed the war-cry of the Macfarlanes.

The reputation of this clan was not far behind the Macgregors as far as desperate courage and mad savagery count. Their headquarters were at first on the Isle of Inveruglas, just near the outflow of that stream into the loch; then they moved to the Brownies' Island, doubtless finding the near neighbourhood of their hereditary enemies, the men of Lorn, too dangerous; but subsequently, becoming bolder, they went to Tarbet, and there settled.

The name Tarbet means draw-boat, and the story goes that Haco, King of Norway, in 1263 entered Loch Long, and, sailing up it, made his men drag the long flat-bottomed boats across the isthmus, and launch them on Loch Lomond, in order that he might the more easily attack the people on its shores for plunder.

The next point of interest is the promontory of Luss, which gives its name to Colquhoun of Luss, whose seat is on the next most beautiful wooded promontory at Rossdhu. This family is one of the most ancient on record, being able to trace its ancestry back to the Colquhouns in 1190 and the Lusses in 1150, which two families were united in the main line by the marriage of a Colquhoun with the heiress of Luss about 1368. Mrs. Walford, the well-known novelist, is a scion of this family. The present mansion was built about the end of the eighteenth century, but a fragment of the old ancestral home is still standing. Not far off are Court Hill and Gallows Hill, where the chieftain tried delinquents, and where justice was meted out to them. The slogan of the clan means "Knoll of the willow."

Across the loch, on the opposite side, is Ross Priory, where Scott was staying with his friend Hector Macdonald when he wrote part of *Rob Roy*.

LOCH LOMOND (Looking towards Glen Falloch).

It is one of the largest lakes in Scotland, and forms part of the famous Trossachs round.

The Islands

Just about here we are in a perfect world of islands, some of which—notably Inchmurrin—are preserved as a deer-park. At the south end are the ruins of a castle once inhabited by the Earls of Lennox, who belonged to the Macfarlane clan. Here Isabel, Duchess of Albany, retired when her father, husband, and sons had been executed at Stirling in 1424. Of the other islands, we have the names of Inchchlonaig, meaning the Island of Yew-trees, on which the yews are said to have been planted by Robert Bruce to furnish bows for his archers; Inchtavannach, or Monks' Island; Inchcruin, Round Island; Inchfad, Long Island; and Inchcaillach, the Island of Women, from a nunnery once established here. This is close to the Pier of Balmaha, where is the entrance to a pass over the mountains, a well-known road in the old days of tribal war and bloodshed.

The Wordsworths landed on Inchtavannach, and climbed to the top of it. Here is Dorothy's description: "We had not climbed far before we were stopped by a sudden burst of prospect, so singular and beautiful that it was like a flash of images from another world. We stood with our backs to the hill of the island, which we were ascending, and which shut out Ben Lomond entirely and all the upper part of the lake, and we looked toward the foot of the lake, scattered over with islands, without beginning and without end. The sun shone, and the distant hills were visible—some through sunny mists, others in gloom with patches of sunshine; the lake was lost under the low and distant hills, and the islands lost in the lake, which was all in motion, with travelling fields of light, or dark shadows under rainy clouds. There are many hills, but no commanding eminence at a distance to confine the prospect, so that the land seemed endless as the water.... Immediately under my eyes lay one large flat island bare and green ... another, its next neighbour, was covered with heath and coppice wood, the surface undulating.... These two islands, with Inchtavannach, where we were standing, were intermingled with the water, I might say interbedded, and interveined with it, in a manner that was exquisitely pleasing. There were bays innumerable, straits or passages like calm rivers, land-locked lakes, and, to the main water, stormy promontories."

Not far from Rossdhu, on the west, is the entrance to Glen Fruin, the Glen of Weeping—a sad name, which turned out to be appropriate enough in view of the terrible scenes which happened here.

The Macgregors

The trouble began with the Macgregors. Their clan claimed descent from the third son of Alpine, King of the Scots, who lived about 787, and was therefore known by the alternative name of Clan Alpine. Their savage ways made them hated by their neighbours, and the Earls of Argyll and Breadalbane managed to obtain from the Government a right by charter to a great part of the lands belonging to the unfortunate clan. This, of course, was the signal for a fight to the death.

From the time of Queen Mary onward various warrants were given to the other clans to make war on the unfortunate Macgregors, and to extirpate them as they would vermin. They were not only to be hounded out of existence, but the other clans were forbidden to supply them with the common necessaries of life. The climax was reached in the slaughter of Glen Fruin, which arose in this wise: Two of the Macgregors, being benighted, called at the house of one of the Colquhouns, and asked shelter. This was refused. They accordingly helped themselves to a sheep and supped off mutton, for which it is alleged they offered payment. The Laird of Luss seized them and had them both executed. Then the rest of the clan arose in wrath, and, to the number of three or four hundred strong, marched down to Luss. Sir Humphrey Colquhoun, receiving warning of their advance, called together his clansmen and others, to double the number of the invaders, and advanced to meet them, doing so in Glen Fruin.

The clan of the Macgregors charged the Colquhouns with fury, and, owing to the fact that part of the opposing force was mounted, and that the horses got mired in the boggy ground, they were able, notwithstanding their inferiority of numbers, to get the best of it, whereupon they set upon their flying foes and slaughtered them mercilessly.

The event which, however, lives in memory longest is that of the action of a gigantic Macgregor, called Dugald Ciar Mohr, or the "great mouse-coloured man," who was in charge, as their tutor, of a party of youths from Glasgow. It is said that, excited by the sound of his clansmen shouting their war-cry, or incensed by the remarks of the youths against his clan, he lost his head; anyway, he slew them all in cold blood.

The Clerk's Stone

The great stone called Leck-a-Mhinisteir, the "minister or clerk's stone," is still pointed out as the place where this horrid deed was done, and it is said the stone was bathed red in the blood of the hapless boys. This Dugald was the ancestor of Rob Roy and his tribe.

The terrible song put by Sir Walter Scott into the mouths of the Macgregor boatmen carries with it a wild cry of savagery:

Proudly our pibroch has thrilled in Glen Fruin,

And Bannacha's groans to our slogan replied;

Glen Luss and Rossdhu they are smoking in ruin;

And the best of Loch Lomond lie dead on its side.

Widow and Saxon maid

Long shall lament our raid,

Think of Clan Alpine with fear and with woe;

Lennox and Leven Glen

Shake when they hear again

Roderick vich Alpine dhu! ho feroe!

After this defeat the fury and wrath of the other clans, who were in favour at Court, may be imagined, and the widows of the slain men, to the number of several score, were sent, dressed in deep mourning, and riding upon white palfreys, carrying each her husband's bloody shirt, to demand vengeance of King James VI. on the Macgregors. The Court was then at Stirling, and surely

Stirling never saw a more woesome sight! The vengeance they obtained was all that they could desire, for by an Act of Privy Council, dated April 3, 1603, the name of Macgregor was wiped out of the land, all those who bore it being compelled, under dire penalties, to adopt the name of some other clan; hence it was that Rob Roy was known as Rob Roy Macgregor Campbell. The Macgregors were forbidden to carry any weapons, and were otherwise penalized. The chief, Alistair Macgregor, who had led the fight at Glen Fruin, was seized, and hanged in 1604. Yet, in spite of these and other dire disabilities, the Macgregors continued to be Macgregors in heart, whatever they might call themselves, and held their heads as high as their own crest, a pine-tree. They attached themselves to the cause of King Charles in the Civil Wars, and were subsequently rewarded by the annulling of the Acts and having their rights restored to them.